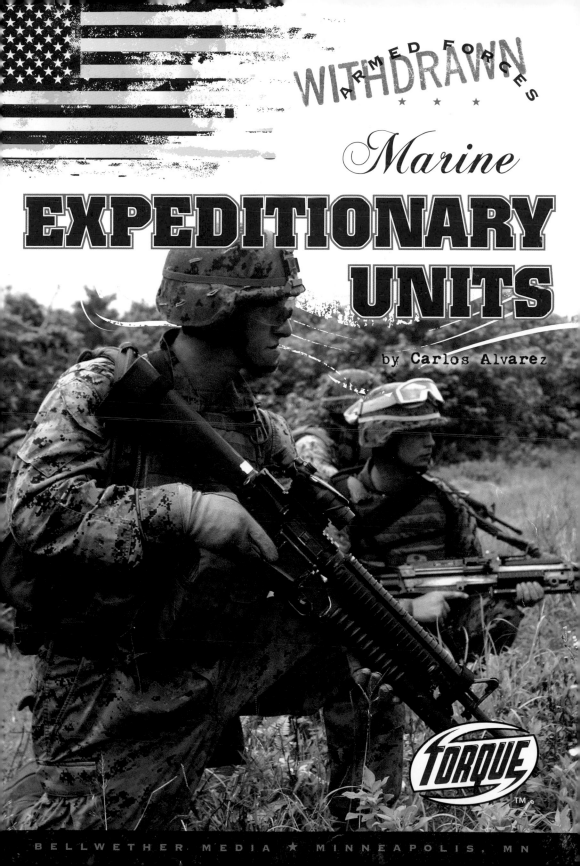

ARMED FORCES

WITHDRAWN

Marine

EXPEDITIONARY UNITS

by Carlos Alvarez

TORQUE™

BELLWETHER MEDIA ★ MINNEAPOLIS, MN

This edition first published in 2010 by Bellwether Media, Inc.

Library of Congress
Alvarez, Carlos, 1968-
  Marine expeditionary units / by Carlos Alvarez.
     p. cm. — (Torque, armed forces)
  Summary: "Amazing photography accompanies engaging
information about Marine Expeditionary Units. The
combination of high-interest subject matter and light text is
intended for students in grades 3 through 7"—Provided by
publisher.
  Includes bibliographical references and index.
  ISBN 978-1-60014-278-9 (hardcover : alk. paper)
  1. United States. Marine Corps—Juvenile literature. 2. Special
forces (Military science)—United States—Juvenile literature. I.
Title.
  VE23.A947 2010
  359.9'631—dc22   2009008497

Printed in the United States of America.

CONTENTS

★ ★ ★

★ ★ ★

Chapter One

WHAT ARE MARINE EXPEDITIONARY UNITS?

 Marine Expeditionary Unit (MEU) is an air-and-ground **task force** of the United States Marine Corps. It specializes in ground combat and **air support**. This means that MEUs can perform **missions** alone. Every resource they need is already in the unit. This allows the units to carry out quick attacks.

MEUs are split into four groups. The Ground Combat
Element (GCE) is the main fighting force. The Aviation
Combat Element (ACE) uses helicopters and planes.
It supports the GCE. The Logistics Combat Element (LCE)
helps the other two complete their missions. The Command
Element (CE) makes the command decisions for the whole
unit. Together, these four parts make up the quickest task
force in the U.S. military.

Chapter Two

WEAPONS AND GEAR

AV-8B Harrier II

M1A1

MEUs use a wide range of vehicles. The units are often based on large United States Navy ships. They use small boats or **amphibious** vehicles to come to shore. They may use armored troop carriers such as the LAV-25 or even the M1A1 main battle tank. Pilots fly AV-8B Harrier jets, AH-1W Super Cobra attack helicopters, and more.

Marine Expeditionary Units were once called Marine Amphibious Units (MAUs).

Amphibious vehicle

M4 carbine

MEUs need effective weapons in combat. Marines carry side arms such as the M16 rifle and the M4 **carbine**. Large machine guns may be mounted to MEU vehicles. Marines also use explosives such as **grenades**, rockets, and anti-tank **missiles** to take out ground vehicles. They use anti-aircraft missiles to shoot down enemy aircraft.

More than half of an MEU's members are in the Battalion Landing Team (BLT). These troops are often the first ones into a battle.

Anti-tank missile

Marines need a variety of other equipment. They wear **camoflauged** uniforms. **Kevlar** helmets protect their heads during combat. They also use **global positioning systems (GPS)** and **night-vision goggles** to complete their missions.

Night-vision goggles

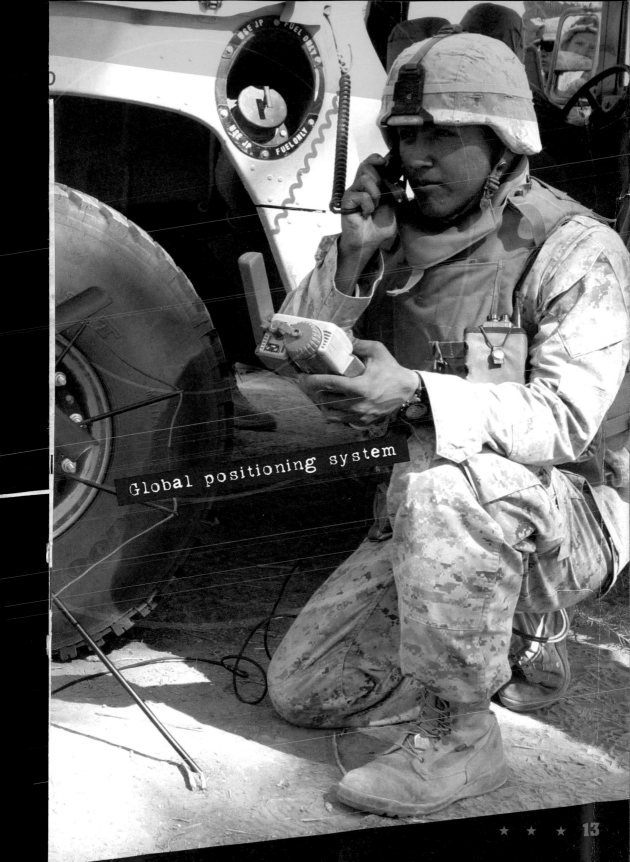

Global positioning system

Chapter Three

LIFE IN A MARINE EXPEDITIONARY UNIT

ach Marine starts out as a recruit in **basic training**. Recruits learn about the Marine Corps. They go through intense physical training. They also learn about weapons and combat tactics. Recruits who complete basic training become Marines.

Marines need more training to be part of an MEU.
They go through a six-month work-up period. The work-up
is sometimes called "**crawl, walk, and run**." Marines learn
more specialized skills during this time. They also continue
their physical training and focus on teamwork.

A unit is ready to **deploy** after the work-up. Each unit contains about 2,200 Marines. They can be stationed anywhere around the world.

They're often based on amphibious ships. They are ready to strike quickly. This ability makes MEUs an important part of the U.S. military.

MEUs are often the first
forces into a combat zone.
They go in to prepare the
way for additional troops.

GLOSSARY

★ ★ ★

air support—the use of aircraft to assist combat forces on the ground

amphibious—able to move easily on land or in water

basic training—the combination of drills, tests, and military training that newly enlisted members of the United States Marine Corps must go through

camouflage—coloring that helps a person or animal blend in with its surroundings

carbine—a short-barreled repeating rifle

crawl, walk, and run—a name for an MEU's work-up period, which includes specialized training in a variety of areas

deploy—to be sent on a military mission

global positioning system (GPS)—a device that uses satellites orbiting Earth to determine a precise position on the globe

grenade—a small explosive that can be thrown or launched with a grenade launcher

Kevlar—a very strong fiber used to make items such as bulletproof vests and armor

missile—an explosive launched at targets on the ground or in the air

mission—a military task

night-vision goggles—a special set of glasses that allow the wearer to see at night

task force—a small, temporary military unit that specializes in performing a specific mission

TO LEARN MORE

★ ★ ★

AT THE LIBRARY

Braulick, Carrie A. *U.S. Marine Expeditionary Units*.
Mankato, Minn.: Capstone, 2006.

David, Jack. *United States Marine Corps*.
Minneapolis, Minn.: Bellwether, 2008.

Green, Michael. *The U.S. Marine Expeditionary
Units at War*. Mankato, Minn.: Capstone, 2004.

ON THE WEB

Learning more about the Marine
Expeditionary Units is as easy as 1, 2, 3.

1. Go to www.factsurfer.com.

2. Enter "Marine Expeditionary Units" into the
   search box.

3. Click the "Surf" button and you will see a list of
   related Web sites.

With factsurfer.com, finding more information is
just a click away.

INDEX

★ ★ ★

The images in this book are reproduced through the courtesy of the United States Department of Defense.